Huff! Puff!

h h h

Written by Catherine Baker

Illustrated by Neil Sutherland, Blue-Zoo and Tony Trimmer

I can run up the hill!

 is fit!

huff! puff!

s is fit ...

... but not as fit as h !

It is a big, BIG hill!

 **s** has got into a mess!

b-u-s , bus!

It is a lot less fuss on
the bus!